THE BEGINNING PROFESSIONAL PUBLISHER

BUSINESS FOR BREAKFAST, VOLUME 2

LEAH R CUTTER

KNOTTED ROAD PRESS

The Beginning Professional Publisher
Business for Breakfast, Volume 2
Copyright © 2015 Leah R Cutter
All rights reserved
Published 2015 by Knotted Road Press
www.KnottedRoadPress.com

ISBN: 978-0692421079

Disclaimer

Never miss a release!

If you'd like to be notified of new releases, sign up for my newsletter.

I only send out newsletters once a quarter, will never spam you, or use your email for nefarious purposes. You can also unsubscribe at any time.
http://www.leahcutter.com/newsletter/

ALSO BY LEAH R CUTTER

The Shadow Wars Trilogy
The Raven and the Dancing Tiger
The Guardian Hound
War Among the Crocodiles

The Clockwork Fairy Kingdom
The Clockwork Fairy Kingdom
The Maker, the Teacher, and the Monster
The Dwarven Wars

Seattle Trolls
The Changeling Troll
The Princess Troll
The Fairy-Bridge Troll

Contemporary Fantasy
The Immortals' War
Siren's Call

The Cassie Stories
Poisoned Pearls
Tainted Waters
Spoiled Harvest

The Chronicles of Franklin

The Popcorn Thief

The Soul Thief

FOREWARD BY BLAZE WARD

The rise of the e-book as a Serious Thing in the early part of this century did something amazingly dangerous to the average writer. It freed them.

The old world was marked by gatekeepers. A handful of editors at a handful of places had nearly-complete dominance over what got published and what got read. Seriously. Fifty years ago there were thousands of mid-sized presses, almost one for every town and a bunch in the big cities.

Now, there are a half-dozen major players. And a bunch of hungry pirates on the horizon. With the rise of the world's biggest bookstore in Seattle, WA, came the tools that let the average writer (average being people like me with no chance in hell of landing a publishing contract, not average in terms of skill as a writer) suddenly put their book up for sale on the interwebs.

Now, you and I can write something and share it with the whole damned planet. Anyone with patience and luck can stumble onto that book, look at the cover, read the blurb, and sniff the fresh electronic ink.

But being able to self-publish means that you need to act like a publisher. Volume One in this series (*The Beginning Professional Writer*) was all about how to write using tricks and techniques honed by pros. And then you publish it. But what does that mean?

It means that you can work as much or as little as you want. Slapdash a cover on it and cough up a hairball for a blurb. Five years ago, that would sell anyway. One might say, in spite of itself. The reading public is HUGE and hungry. Think of a two year old. They don't understand need, but they cry for something to fill them.

That was us. Trying to fill the sea with an eye-dropper.

For several years, it was enough. You could put something up, and someone would buy it.

That won't work anymore.

Why not?

Because in the last year or so, the big TradPub houses realized that they had competition. And they started competing. Their mid-lists were suddenly a gold mine. Prices came down from stupid to affordable.

You are now competing with billion dollar conglomerates.

Let that sink in for a moment. You, in the comfort of your front room, in your sweat pants and fuzzy bunny slippers, are able to compete with a billion dollar publishing house.

The old joke is that on the internet, nobody knows you are a dog.

Here, nobody knows you are a small shop publisher. If you act like a professional, turn out good stories, wrapped in pretty packages, people will buy your stuff just as readily, maybe more so.

Volume One was all about answers to questions you weren't sure about. This volume is all about questions themselves. Leah doesn't know what will work for you. Neither do I. And I'm damned sure certain you don't, either. You don't have to. You have to start asking questions: How big do I want to be? How do I schedule things far enough out to get pretty books in the right hands? How do I make sure they find them?

And this book will be out of date quickly. I know a mid-size publisher, a serious player in the business, who can't even tell, six months out, what the market will be doing, because right now, spring 2015, everything is in flux.

But you've got an ally. Leah publishes a half-dozen writers, herself included, in a stupidly-wide mix of genre. She's thought about what it is she is doing, plans to do, wants to do. This is your chance to start asking yourself what you want to be when you grow up.

The future is as crazy, as golden, as serious, as silly as you are willing to commit to.

What's stopping you?

Blaze Ward
April 2015

INTRODUCTION

Congratulations! You're considering publishing your own work! Or perhaps you're already publishing.

This is not going to be a step-by-step guide in how to publish.

Instead, this book is going to make sure that you know which questions to ask.

It's been my experience that when I start to learn a new topic—and I mean something really new—I don't even know enough to ask questions. Or the right questions.

This book assumes that while you know some things about publishing (perhaps you've even published things before) there's things you don't know, things you don't even know that you need to ask about or think about.

This book isn't going to answer those questions. Instead, it's going to direct you to areas you need to think about, to at least let you know that you need to ask questions about a topic.

There won't be homework, per se, with some of the chapters. But I will tell you that you'll need to do research.

For example: the number of platforms where you can publish ebooks is continually changing. Platforms start, become the hottest new thing, then begin to have problems and publishers move away from using them. If I gave you a list of where you could publish your ebooks, it would be out of date five minutes after I wrote it.

You'll need to do your own research.

Another example. Covers. Tastes change. Look at book covers that were considered modern and hip and cool in the 1970s. They look horribly dated to us now.

The covers you do today will look great today.

Will they still be considered great five years from now? Or will they look dated?

So sometimes I will tell you to go and see what is current in your genre *today*.

Genre

There are some things that are universal, such as organizing your computer, your publishing schedule, etc.

Some things are dictated by your genre.

For example: If you're writing literary fiction, your covers, keywords, and pricing are all genre dependent.

As a writer, you don't have to be aware of any of this.

But this isn't a book for writers.

This is a book for publishers.

And as a publisher, you'll need to study genre. (There will be a lot more on genre later.)

Different Hats

I will emphasize this a few times in the book because it's that important.

Your publishing business is a separate business from your writing.

You should have separate checking accounts for your writing business and your publishing business. (More details later).

Writing income (such as, selling to a magazine or an anthology, or a speaking fee, or teaching fees) should all be separate from the publishing income, what people pay you for your books. If you're in the US, you may have to pay different tax rates on the different types of income. It will be much easier if you keep the two separate.

My publishing company, for example, also provides production services (such as cover design, epub formatting, etc.) and that income must be tracked separately.

As a writer, write the books of your heart. Write what makes you giggle. What draws you back to the keyboard, such that you don't need discipline or an external system to get you to write.

After you have finished writing, and revising, and copyedits, and everything else, only then do you put on your publisher hat. Never before. Don't let other people (and particularly not the market!) into your writing office.

However, you need to understand the market and genre and a whole bunch of other things once you've put on that publishing hat.

My Burgeoning Publishing Empire

Let me show it to you!

I do understand that my path is different than what most people choose. However, I'm really happy with how it's all turned out.

I started my publishing company back in 2011. I was attending the first class down on the Oregon Coast, taught by Dean Wesley Smith, called, "Think Like a Publisher."

I published a couple of short stories during that class, and learned a whole bunch.

Then I stopped publishing.

This is *very* typical, and happens to most writers, particularly those of us who have been raised in traditional publishing.

I don't know why it's so overwhelming. But it is.

I believe there was still some part of my brain rebelling over publishing my own material. *This isn't how publishing works! It isn't supposed to be this easy! Anyone can now find my books!* Etc.

After a few months I got over myself and started the *Baker's Dozen* challenge, in part to get me to start publishing again. The challenge was to write, edit, copyedit, create a cover, format, and publish a short story every week.

I started writing each story on Monday and published every Sunday. (I missed one week by a single day because I was sick. I still count it as a win.)

It was a great challenge for me. I developed some wonderful

stories (that have later gone on to inspire other stories or novels). It also got me in the habit of publishing.

I always knew that I'd like to publish other people. Eventually my fiancé came into my life, and I started publishing his works.

Then I published a chapbook by his mother, all about growing up in a carnival in the mid-west in the 1940s and 50s. Then some erotica by a friend. Then a business book written by a different friend. And it just kept going from there.

Knotted Road Press has over 100 titles, and publishes six authors. In 2015, I plan on publishing another 40 titles, and may have eight writers. Knotted Road Press will probably have over 200 titles by 2016.

Not everyone has or wants that kind of volume. But I have published a lot. And I'd like to share my experience with you.

Unique Business

As an artist, I intuitively understand that what I create is unique and different than what anyone else has created. I have my own Voice, I tell my own stories.

I think this helps me with my business. My publishing business is also unique, different than everyone else's. What I decide to do for my business may not be the right decision for your business.

Everyone will have different skills that they bring to their business. For example, I know some writers who are good at Facebook. They talk about their dogs, and their work, and sometimes they also have these brilliant posts about the book they just published. For them, that kind of active marketing is easy and fun, and is part of every book marketing plan.

Another publisher might write great blurbs, but decides to get professional help on covers. Or vice-versa.

What you do for your business in terms of marketing and general infrastructure will be different than anyone else.

Embrace your uniqueness.

For me, that's a huge part of the fun of being a small press. I get to decide what's right for me and my business. I could be wrong, but then I have no one else to blame but me. And I like that as well, because I can always learn, and can always do better the next time.

In Conclusion

Like the previous volume of *Business for Breakfast, Volume 1: The Beginning Professional Writer*, this book is written more for the artist than the business person. I'll try to keep the terms simple and understandable for those of you who are new to all of this.

Every chapter is also short, meant to be consumed in a short period, say, while you're eating breakfast. Thus the name

Perhaps you'll decide that publishing (and doing it right) is just too much work. That's fair. There are people who don't enjoy publishing, who decide to partner with other professionals to get all the details right, because they would rather be writing.

Me? I like both the business and the creative sides of writing.

I hope you decide to join me on this ride.

Leah Cutter
April 2015

CHAPTER ONE

Initial Decisions

Congratulations! You're considering publishing your own work! Or perhaps you're already publishing, and just want to go back over the basics.

This chapter will walk you through the initial steps.

You And Who?

One of the first things for you to think about is whether you want to publish just yourself or if you're also going to publish other people.

Maybe you don't want to be a big publisher. Maybe you just have a mother-in-law with a fascinating story that you want to capture. Maybe you have a friend who has this collection of poetry that you'd like to publish for them. Maybe you have other projects of the heart that you'd like for the world to see.

Or perhaps you just want to publish yourself, and you'll never touch someone else's manuscript. It's your House, and yours alone.

Or possibly you have kind of a head for business, and you've always wanted to be a publisher. So you plan on being a bigger press, and working with many artists.

One of your first decisions will be to figure out your size, both current and future.

I started off knowing that I wanted to publish other people. I knew that I have a good head for business, and that I liked business.

It still took me three years before I added another writer. I needed to make sure that all the aspects of my business, in in particular, the accounting, were in place before I more than doubled the complication of adding another person.

Adding one more person after the first didn't triple the complication. I knew it would grow more complicated, but once the infrastructure was in place, it just meant a bit more work.

Changing Size

You may not know that you want to publish other people. Perhaps you haven't done any publishing yet and so you don't know if you're going to like it or not.

Or perhaps you think you'll be a bigger publisher, only to find out just how much work it is, and decide to publish only yourself.

While that initial decision is important, it's also important to realize that you can change your mind later.

My advice would be to start small and grow from there. Get your toes wet, then your feet, then decide if you want to move further into the water.

The Name Game

Once you've some idea of your size, if you're going to be just strictly you or a stable or writers, you get the fun job of picking a name for your press.

As a writer/artist, you already understand that names are important. Part of the name game, though, is to match the name of your business with your plans.

I would suggest that you choose a more serious, professional name. On the one hand, it might be funny if you became a best seller and during an interview, made the interviewer have to say the name of your publisher: Mac-Fluffy-Snuckums Press.

On the other hand, if you do write a best-selling novel, you'd like people to take you seriously. That will be easier if the name of your publishing house sounds professional.

If you really want to name your publishing business after your cats, possibly just use their initials: MFS Press.

Another thing to think about: choose a name that doesn't reflect a single genre.

Perhaps you only write science fiction, and so you want your press to reflect that, and plan on calling it Spaceship Monkeys Publications.

I would caution against this. You're limiting yourself with that kind of name. While it's indicative of what you're writing today, as an artist, you're also limiting your growth. Who's to say that you might not read some fantasy book and decide, "I can do better than that." Then go on to to love those books and become a best-selling author in that genre.

I'm not saying choose a bland, generic name. But choose one that will allow you to write in all genres, that will still fit ten, twenty, fifty years from now.

Once you choose a name, the internet will be your friend. You must do searches on that name, both how you're spelling it as well as alternate spellings. You may have picked an absolutely awesome name —only to find out that someone else is already using it. So be sure to look around before making your final decision.

You may also want to check with other people about the name you've chosen, people who are in different social circles. They may see something about your name, or know that it's disrespectful slang.

Separation

You have a great name for your publisher. You have some idea of who you want to publish, the size you want to get to.

Now, you need to start thinking of that publisher as a separate entity.

It is a separate business from your writing. It will generate separate income.

You need to set up a separate bank account for your publisher. This will make it very easy, later, when it comes time to do your taxes, as your income for your business has been separate from your other income.

In addition, you need this information before you start setting up accounts with distributors.

Before I could open a bank account for my publishing business in Washington State, in the US, I needed to get a business license. You will need to check with the laws of your country/state/province to see what's required as part of your banking laws.

Some people will tell you that if you live in the US, you should also get an Employee Identification Number (EIN). This acts as your business social security number. You would use it with your distributors, on all contracts you sign, etc.

Until you actually form a corporation, I would advise against doing this, at least initially. If you do grow to the size that you need to incorporate, having an existing EIN becomes a problem, not an asset. And you don't really need it to start off with, anyway.

Web Presence

Everyone will tell you that you need to get a web site and use your publisher's name as the domain, such as www.FlyingPinkMonkeys.com.

In general, this is good advice. Let me explain why.

Suppose you want to submit your work to a review site such as Publisher's Weekly.

Publisher's Weekly is used to dealing with traditional publishers, not authors. They expect to receive books from *publishers.*

This means, as part of your cover letter, you list the name of your publishing company, as well as the web site. You need to look like a business to them if you want them to take you seriously.

You may want to set up someone as your publisher as well. That way, all correspondence comes from someone who is not you. This could be a friend of yours, who agrees to be your publisher. Or it could be just a persona you assume.

Do you need to spend a lot of time and effort on your publisher's website up front? Not necessarily.

If you never, ever, *ever,* intend to publish people other than yourself, you can have a very simple publisher website with a static page, links to your author website, as well as a contact form.

If you may decide to publish people other than yourself, or you have open pen names that you publish under, you should probably start building your publishing website as soon as you begin publishing. It's easier to just add to an existing site than to have to build it from scratch when you have a dozen books.

Another site that you need to build (or make sure that your authors build) are your author website or sites. This is not the same as the author's Twitter account, Facebook, Tumblr, etc.

The website/blog may or may not be where the writer, primarily communicates with their fans. Building up that web presence is for author, not the publisher. However, as a publisher, you might be encouraging your authors to build up their social media sites.

Your author site preferably has the author name as the domain (www.LeahCutter.com). This site contains information about the author's books.

The landing page for the author site should contain the following:

- What's just been released
- What's coming
- How to contact the author
- Signing up for the author's newsletter
- Social media links
- Upcoming events

These are the pieces of information that readers want to know. Tell them about your cats in your social media posts. Tell them about your books and your business up front.

If you write in series, you might want to create a separate page for each series, so readers know what order the books are in. If you have a lot of books, you might want to create a FAQ to direct readers to the book they should start with.

Some writers choose to put the majority of their effort into their author site, and just use the publishing site for correspondence and for publishing. Their publisher's site is static, with links to their author site as well as a page for retailers.

If you decide to sell books through your website, I would recommend doing that on your publishing site, and keep the businesses separated.

If you're publishing more than one person, you need to put more effort into your publishing site. If you're also offering services, such as editing, cover design, career advice, I would recommend doing that through your publishing house, and keep your writing separate.

There are many different ways to run a business. You get to choose how to show yours to the world.

Web Hosts

Talk with other writers to find out what they are using. Make sure it's an actual web host. There are a lot of fake services out there.

Whatever service you use, I cannot recommend strongly enough to use whatever privacy service your web host offers. (If your web host doesn't offer a privacy service, go find another web host.)

Let me explain what a privacy service does.

When you register your domain name, you need to fill in information, such as your name, address, phone number, etc.

That information is now public record. Anyone can access it.

That is, unless you use your web host's privacy service.

If you use your web host's privacy service, a casual inquiry will show the web host's information, not yours. (For those of you more technical, it's what's returned with a WHOIS command.)

Perhaps it doesn't matter to you now that your address and phone number are easily available.

What happens if you write the next Harry Potter book? You might not want to move, but you might have to if anyone with a computer can figure out where you live.

Assume success. Plan for victory.

Choosing Partners

As part of your plan, you should decide which distributors you're going to use for your work, such as (for today): Amazon, Draft2Digital, iTunes, Createspace, Audible, etc.

Make a list. Then do some investigation. There are horror stories about every single one of those platforms.

Which ones will you choose? Feel free to go against the trend, as long as you go in with your eyes open. All those different platforms are businesses. Sometimes you have to put up with unpleasantness in order to do business with a partner.

Decide your pain points. Do your research. Read the terms of service for each and every partner.

Then, and only then, set up accounts with them.

In Conclusion

Here's a brief list of the steps:

- Decide who you want to publish.
- Choose a professional sounding name for your publishing house.
- Apply for a business license in your state.
- Use the business license to set up business accounts with your bank of choice.
- Investigate distribution partners for your books.
- Use your business bank accounts to set up publishing accounts with the various distributors.

And remember: your web presence is important. Choose a good host and use their privacy service.

CHAPTER TWO

Production 101

You've chosen your publishing name, set up your bank accounts, chosen the distributors that you want to publish with. Right?

Now what?

This chapter will walk you through the basics of what's called *Production*, that is, taking a finished manuscript through all the steps necessary to get it ready for publication.

Other chapters will go into more depth about some of these steps.

First Step

Take off your writing hat.

Seriously. If you're not physically wearing a hat, at least mime taking off that writing hat.

Now, put on your publishing hat. Again, mime the action if you don't actually have a cool fedora that you use to get you in the mood for managing your publishing empire.

Go through that physical motion again, literally miming taking off one hat and putting on a different hat, whenever you find yourself thinking like a writer.

You're no longer a writer. Now, you're a publisher.

This is an essential first step. You'll break this rule a lot when you first start. I know I did. Eventually, however, you'll get the hang of it.

So put on your publisher's hat, and let's go.

Determine the Genre

Choose a project. Just pick one to start with. I would advise starting with a short story—it's shorter, and theoretically, it will be easier to go through all the production steps with a shorter project.

First thing that you, *as the publisher*, need to determine is the genre for this piece.

The genre will determine so many other things about this piece, including the cover, the style of blurb that you write, the keywords, the pricing, where you distribute it, what markets you might send it to for reviews, etc.

So figure out the genre.

Sure, you might be writing some fancy sort of time-travel western that blurs a bunch of genres.

You still must pick just one.

Decide, *as the publisher*, if the book is 51% western and only 49% some other thing.

Why is determining the genre so important? Many reasons, but the first is discoverability. Readers have been trained to look for books by genre. Readers classify themselves as mystery readers, or literary snobs, or science fiction addicts.

Genre is strictly a marketing tool. It has no bearing on what or how you write.

Determining a genre is a publishing and marketing decision. You have your publishing hat on. This is *not* a writing decision. You are not currently the writer, remember?

You should also be aware of which genres trump other genres. For example, if you write a romance that follows all of the conventions of romance, and then you throw in robots, you may not have a romance anymore. Readers may consider it science fiction now, because science fiction tends to trump every other genre.

(If you want an absolutely excellent class to learn about genre, I can't recommend Dean Wesley Smith's Genre workshop enough.)

If you *as the publisher* can't determine what genre a piece is, give it to a trusted reader to tell you what genre they think it's in.

It's okay if you get it wrong. You can always go back and change everything.

Most writers never know what genre they write in. Even when they think they know, they're wrong.

So spend the time learning about genre and pick the right one. (More about genre later in *Chapter Four: Basic Marketing, Part One.*)

Form

For my publishing house, the rule tends to be that any piece longer than 10,000 words gets a print edition.

Other publishing houses choose to produce print editions for every book.

Others choose to produce print editions only for works longer than 40,000.

Perhaps you also want to produce an audio version of this book.

Perhaps you'll also do a series of blog posts regarding this book.

Maybe this book will only be available in print, and not in ebook format.

Or maybe this is the book you'll use to try that new serialization platform.

It is up to you.

But you should decide what form(s) the book is going to be produced in.

Dates

It's difficult to create a publication schedule when you're first starting out and you have no idea how long the production is going to take.

Remember, however, that the production schedule is always written in pencil. Or on erasable white-marker boards. Or in your special, separate, Google calendar that you use to keep track of all your deadlines (very easy to move those dates!)

Production schedules *change.* Constantly. Be prepared for tossing out everything you were planning on doing in a quarter because something else fell into your lap. It happens more frequently than you think.

However, it's considerably easier to change an *existing* schedule and to move things around then to have everything be amorphous and undefined.

So pick a date for when you want to publish this single piece you've chosen.

If you're producing a print version, add six weeks. You'll need that time to review the proof without having to pay crazy shipping costs.

If you're only producing an ebook, give yourself at least three weeks, possibly more, because there's a learning curve with all of this.

Now, write those dates down. Shoot for having a single date for all the forms of a book, but be realistic about it. Sometimes a different form for a book will come out later.

They can change. They probably will.

But write down the dates so you have something to shoot for.

More about building a production schedule in *Chapter Six, The Production Schedule is Written in Pencil.*

Marketing

What level of marketing support are you going to provide for this book?

Not all books receive the same level of marketing. Nor should they.

As a publisher, you have limited time and money. (Remember, you wear another hat, that is, a writing hat. Time you spend marketing is time you are *not* spending writing.)

You may choose to do a minimal amount of marketing for a project that's not the same as your regular genre and what you're best known for writing. Or perhaps it's the first book in a new series. Or maybe it's just a short story.

Whatever the reason, it's *your* choice. Make a decision as a publisher.

More about basic marketing in *Chapter Four, Basic Marketing, Part One,* and *Chapter Five, Basic Marketing, Part Two.*

Doing the Work

Now that you have the planning out of the way, you get to actually do the work.

The steps include:

- Getting the piece copyedited if it hasn't been.

NOTE: There are some writers who can copyedit their own work. Me? I'll misspell my own name given a chance. I always have someone else copyedit my work.

- Choose your marketing plan.
- Write the blurb, blurbs, and/or ads.
- Create the appropriate covers. You'll need a separate cover for each form, such as print, ebook, audio, etc.
- Create the ads.
- Format the piece for print.
- Format the piece for ebook.
- Send to distributors.
- Send ads to marketers.
- Bask in the glory of having published a book!

Of course, some of these steps contain a lot more steps, which I'll go into later. (Much of this will be covered in *Chapter Six, The Production Schedule is Written in Pencil.*)

The steps aren't difficult. They are work, however. There's a learning curve. But it will get easier as you do more project.

In Conclusion:

Here are the three things you need to remember about basic production work:

- Take off your writing hat and put on your publishing hat.
- Determine the genre for a piece, then decide the formats and the dates.

- Do the work and publish that book!

CHAPTER THREE

File Organization 101

When you first start publishing, you might have your books scattered in different folders, and your blurbs someplace else, as well as a separate folder for reviews, and links, and keywords, and...

This sort of organic organization works when you only have a few books.

What happens when you have ten? Or twenty? Or more?

It is better to start with some level of organization, and to move your files now, because having them scattered and not being sure where to find something will make any updates to those books time consuming later.

This chapter will cover basic organization for your *publishing*. I assume that you have a completely separate computer, or at the very least, a separate file system for your *writing*.

NOTE: Do not mix the two! Keep the writing files separate from the publishing files! You have your publishing hat on, not your writing hat!

File Structure—Top Level

I know, I know. *File Structure.* Scary words. But I would advise starting at the top, with the highest level of things that need to be organized, then working down from there.

And the top level for most people and computers is files. (I am going to assume that you understand what a file is on a computer system. If you don't, go and look it up. However, the rest of this chapter may be beyond you.)

What do you tend to write? Do you write in series? Do you tend to write all stand-alone books? Or something in between?

I'm going to propose a few different organization structures for your files. You get to choose the one that works for you.

I tend to write stand-alone novels, as well as stand-alone short stories. The top of my file structure looks like this:

- Collections
- Non_Fiction
- Novels
- Stories

I also have other folders, such as zz_Guidelines, zz_Icons, zz_Graphics. Note that these all start with zz, so that they'll appear at the bottom of the list of my files.

NOTE: I do not use spaces when creating folder or file names. I would advise to NEVER use spaces for either folder or file names. While modern computers can find items that have spaces in the names, they still sometimes mess up.

Suppose you write primarily in series. All your short stories, collections, as well as your novels are in one or more series.

You might instead want a different structure, named by series title. For example:

- Clockwork_Kingdom
- Franklin_Chronicles
- Shadow_Wars
- When_The_Moon

What if you write a combination of the two? Some series, some stand alones? Maybe you want to organize then by both series name, as well as by character names. For example:

- Alexandria_Station
- Brak
- Doyle
- Kaleph
- Suren

Really, you just need to pick a structure that works for you, that will help you find things easily.

And remember, you can always switch your structure around. It takes some time, but a new structure that's easier to navigate will save you time in the long run.

File Structure—Lower Levels

So you have your top level structure. I have intermediate structures under the top level, because again, I write mostly stand-alone pieces. For example, under the big category of "Stories" I have an alphabet system:

- A-H
- I-M
- N-S
- T-Z

It's up to you if you decide you're going to start with an alphabet system, or if you'll move to one later when you start having screen after screen filled with stories. I actually started with merely three divisions of the alphabet and had to change over to four because each list was getting too long. At some point, I may have to it change to five.

Underneath that, I list items by title, and frequently, an abbreviated title—just the first word. I tend to leave out the "The" or "A" and just go with the regular title.

For example:

- Black_Pearl
- Cold_Comfort
- Curious_Case
- Doom
- Golden_Charms

Curious_Case is actually *The Curious Case of Rabbit and the Temple Goddess*, but I don't need all of that for a file name. Just Curious_Case is enough for me to know what that story is.

Instead of story titles, you may want to organize by character name, if that isn't at the upper level. Again, it's up to you.

Pick a structure, though, and implement it.

After you have that basic top-level structure, what goes into each of those folders tends to be similar. I tend to have the following folders, where *Title* is the name of the story or book, under each of the folders:

- *Title*_Book—contains the files for doing the ebook, including the final versions of the .epub and .mobi files. Depending on how I generated the ebooks, it may also contain the final PDF of the print book.
- *Title*_Cover—contains all the cover files. I name them appropriately, such as *Title*_cover_ebook, *Title*_cover_print, *Title*_cover_businessCard, etc. This file may contain another file, ZZ_*Title*_Covers_Old, if I've been playing around with a lot of art, or if I've rebranded or recovered the book.
- *Title*_Print—contains the files for doing the print edition if I haven't generated the print book at the same time as the ebooks.
- *Title*_Audio—contains the files necessary for doing the audio version. This file generally contains notes about the character and script, as well as corrections that need to be made to the final version.

In addition, I have the following files at the top level:

- Info_*Title*
- ISBN_*Title*
- *Title*_Master

The master file is the final version of the story. (Remember, your *writing* versions of the file are located someplace else.)

The ISBN file contains the ISBNs you've assigned to the property.

Then there's that mysterious info file. This is where the magic happens.

Info File

What kind of information goes into the info file? All kinds of things.

I cannot stress this enough—having an info file for every story (novel, poem, song, etc.) will save you so much time in the long run as you build up your number of properties.

I put the following into the info file:

- Book tag line (such as, "A post-apocalyptic fairy tale" or "Sometimes it takes more than eyes to see.")
- Short blurb
- Long blurb
- Keywords
- Number of pages of print book
- Pull-quotes from reviews
- ISBN numbers of similar books (for something like LibraryThing reviews)

Building this file *before* you publish a book can save you an immense amount of time when you fill out the information on each distributor's website. Particularly if you then expand to another platform, later. You'll have all the information in one, dependable, recurring place.

If you end up making changes to a blurb (because some platforms need a shorter blurb, and maybe your original went over the limit) be sure to update the info file with the final version.

But wait! There's one more important structure to build.

Links File

I have another folder at the top level of my computer that I call Writing_Biz. In that folder, I have additional folders for all the reports I pull down from distributors, contracts I've signed, my bios for different genres, etc.

In addition, I have a spreadsheet that contains links to where I've published every single book.

I have a separate, duplicate sheet for each author.

The first column contains the title of the work. Again, I tend to drop the "The" and "A" from the title.

The second column contains the date I published the title. If there's a second edition of a book, I'll list that second date as well.

In the following columns, I list distributors, one for each column, such as Amazon, Kobo, Book View Café, Draft2Digital, iTunes, etc. In that column for that title, I copy and paste the direct link to that book on that platform.

The spreadsheet is pretty big at this point—under my name alone, I have close to one hundred and fifty titles.

But it saves me time when I need to find a link to a book because I always know where those links are.

I find it much easier to keep those links together, in a single file, rather than separate them out into the info file.

Your Mileage May Vary (YMMV). Find a structure that works for you.

In Conclusion

Here are the three things to remember about file organization:

- Keep your publishing files separate from your writing files.
- Organizing now will save you *so much time* in the long run.
- Develop a link file to keep track of all your titles.

CHAPTER FOUR

Basic Marketing, Part One

There are two types of marketing:

- Active
- Passive

Active marketing, such as posting on Facebook, sending books to reviewers, purchasing ads, blogging, do *not* have to be the majority of your marketing budget or time. If you're a writer, remember that marketing time is not writing time. Sometimes, it's more important to focus on writing the next book.

However, there are a lot of *passive* marketing things that you can do, that will sell your books over time.

They don't feel like marketing, in part, because we tend to think of marketing as that shouting in your face *Buy My Book!*

But they can be just as effective. Depending on the project, they may be *more* effective.

This chapter will cover some of what you can do to *passively* market your book. These are things you do once, then don't touch again for a year or more.

Genre Basics

Identifying the correct genre for your books is a great way to market it. Putting it in the correct category increases the chances that someone will find your book.

If you don't understand what genre is, or know much about genre, again, I'd recommend Dean's class.

This is going to be a very high-level overview to help get you started. You will need to study it on your own.

Genres include (and are not limited to):

- Literary
- Science Fiction
- Fantasy
- Mystery
- Romance
- Thriller
- Horror
- Non-Fiction
- Children
- Young Adult
- Erotica

Each of these genres contain subgenres. For example, there are many different subgenres of mystery, such as:

- Amateur sleuth
- Cozy
- Hard-boiled
- Noir
- Woman sleuth

Each subgenre has its own conventions. As a publisher, you need to look at a property and be able to place it correctly. A writer can break a few of the conventions of a subgenre, but you must know which ones.

So you must study genre.

Where can you start your learning about genres?

A good place to start is with the BISAC, or *basic industry subject and category* lists. They're updated every year, so you'll want to do an internet search and find the most recent list.

But this is just a starting place. Another place to look are the Amazon's categories.

If you go to Amazon, and Shop by Department, Books, Kindle Books, on the left-hand side of the page that displays, you can traverse genres and subgenres.

NOTE: The categories listed there aren't complete. There are many more subgenres and sub-sub-genres that you can choose for your books.

I go into more details about Amazon categories and sub-categories in *Chapter Ten, Distributing and Branding.*

One other item to note: Genre is one of those things that changes over the years.

For example, there used to be a very popular genre called Sword and Sorcery fiction. It would now be classified as Action & Adventure. What used to qualify for a thriller would no longer pass muster with today's readers—those stories would now be classified under suspense, or mystery.

So you must study genre. It's one of your most important passive marketing tools. Then make sure that you get your book into the right genre.

Cover Basics

After you've identified the genre for a property, your next most important piece of passive marketing is getting a kick-ass cover.

One thing to be aware of: as independent publishing grows, so does the skill set. Back at the dawn of time (more than five years ago) an independent publisher could slap any kind of cover on a title and it would do well. There wasn't much material available, so if you told a good story, it didn't matter as much how you marketed it.

These days, it's growing more and more difficult to tell the difference between a cover produced by a large New York publisher and an independent press.

When I first started publishing back in 2011, I thought that all writers could create great covers.

I've now changed my mind. A writer must have a good eye to be able to create great covers, an artist's eye. Most writers can do good or adequate covers.

However, that isn't good enough anymore, not with the proliferation of material out there. Unfortunately, most authors don't have that artist's eye, and can't take their covers to the next level.

What makes a great cover? The answer, of course, is that it depends on the genre. What makes a great fantasy cover would make a horrible thriller cover. A great mystery cover would make a horrible romance cover. Etc.

After you've determined the genre for a property, I would recommend going to a bookstore and looking at covers in that genre. (I would also recommend looking at different genres, to start getting an idea of what conventions a genre uses.)

Make sure that you're looking at recently published books and not reprints of older books with older covers. In addition, make sure that you're looking at trade paperbacks, the bigger books, not at the mass market paperbacks.

Amazon is another place to go and look at covers. I would recommend specifying print books as part of your search. That way you're looking primarily at traditionally published covers, and at small presses who know what they're doing.

You might also look at the top forty books for a subgenre, such as Hard Science Fiction or Cozy Mystery. These are the books that are selling a certain number per day. They've done some of the passive marketing correctly.

In general, the following items make for a good cover:

- Small print, such as the book tag, author tag, review quote, etc. You can't read that text when the book cover is displayed at thumbnail size. But it's one of the large distinguishing factors between amateurs and professionals.
- Cover looks good at both thumbnail and larger size. Some genres (such as literary) currently have the author name tiny, so that you can't see it even at the larger size. That

doesn't make it a bad cover, that just means it's in a particular genre. But the cover, itself, looks good both at thumbnail as well as larger size.

- Elements all fit together. The name doesn't overpower the title, or vice-versa. The whole cover looks as though it fits together. Nothing jars the eye in an unpleasant way. Listen to your subconscious mind. (If you find yourself still puzzling over a cover a week after you've "finished" it, something's probably wrong with it that you need to fix.)

Then there are genre specific things, such as mysteries tend to use photos on the cover while fantasy tends to use non-photo-realistic artwork, romance of all varieties tends to have people on the covers, etc. But you'll need to study genre to find out what's current in your field.

Another place to study covers: The Book Designer (thebookdesigner.com) holds a monthly contest for ebook covers. Look at those, and more importantly, read the analysis he does of every cover. I disagree with his opinions frequently, but it's a good starting education.

Another place to study covers: sign up for traditional publisher's newsletter, those who publish in the genres you are publishing. Once a week, they'll send you a newsletter that contains the latest covers. It will take you five minutes a week, but after a couple months, you'll start to get a feel for what's currently popular in terms of covers and what isn't.

Another place to study covers: Allyson Longueira, the publisher for WMG Publishing, does a couple of lectures on covers. (http://www.DeanWesleySmith.com/lecture-series/)

But I have no talent as an artist, and I'm going to have to buy all my covers. So why should I study covers?

Because you may have an artist who creates absolutely amazing romance covers and not have the first clue about how to create an urban fantasy cover.

As a publisher, you need to make sure that your books are placed in the correct genre. You can't rely on the artist to know what's correct for a genre. You need to know that. You'll have to direct the artist who creates the covers, to make sure that they're appropriate.

Get help from experts, but remember that the final choice and decision is yours.

Warning: Covers are one of the place where you really need to make sure that you're wearing your publishing hat and NOT your writing hat. Do not fall into the author problem by insisting that the elf on the cover must have blue hair and a certain look. All you need is something that indicates that it's fantasy, that describes the right subgenre, mood, or tone. Don't dwell too much on the details. Nail genre and get the rest of the details close enough.

Blurbs

After determining your genre and obtaining a kick-ass cover, blurbs are your third most important piece of passive marketing.

Think about it this way: A reader walks into a bookstore. They go to the section of the bookstore that has their favorite genre (mystery, science fiction, photography books, etc.) They pull a book off the shelf, drawn by the cover.

Then they flip the book over to read the blurb on the back of the book.

Blurbs don't tend to rely as much on genres. There are a few basics to remember about blurbs:

Blurbs are *marketing material.* Take off your writer hat and put on your publisher hat. You don't want to tell the plot (this happened, and then this happened, and then this happened.) You do want to tell the *story* and just give a hint of what's to come.

Blurbs are written in third-person present tense. Never use a passive verb (eliminate all varieties of the verb "To Be.") Only describe what happens in the first chapter of a book, not the entire book. Leave the reader wanting to know what happens next. If you telegraph the entire plot in the blurb, why should the reader pick up the book? They already know what's going to happen.

There are many types of blurbs: The back cover of the print book. The description field of an ebook. The short description that some distributors insist upon (less than 100 words). The teaser you put on the back of a business card. Etc.

Remember, however, to keep all the versions of a blurb for a book in a single file.

To learn more about blurbs, take Dean Wesley Smith's class on Writing Sales Copy. (http://www.DeanWesleySmith.com/online-workshops/)

In Conclusion

Here are the three things to remember about basic marketing:

- There's both *passive* and *active* marketing. Getting the passive marketing correct will make selling your books easier.
- Genre determines most everything, so figuring out the genre for your book is key.
- Covers and blurbs are your next most important passive marketing. You need to study them so you'll get them right.

CHAPTER FIVE

Basic Marketing, Part Two

As discussed in the previous chapter, there are two forms of marketing:

- *Active*
- *Passive*

The previous chapter discussed some of the more important passive marketing that you can do.

This chapter will discuss a few more passive marketing techniques, as well as some of the active marketing that you can do.

Publish the Next Book

Think about your bookstore as a bakery.

A customer walks in. There's a single type of cookie available. The rest of the shelves are bare and empty. There aren't any cakes in the display cases, no scones, no pies, nothing.

Just the single type of cookie.

Maybe you'll have a lot of customers who like that flavor of cookie. Yay! Go you.

However, once your customers finish reading your One True Book, what are they going to read next? You have else nothing to offer them.

You need to add other products to your bakery to make customers return to your store.

So build a bakery of products. Maybe you're only publishing yourself, and you write primarily in a series, so you'll have fourteen different types of chocolate chip cookies, as well as seven types of oatmeal cookies, and nine types of macaroons.

Or maybe you publish other people, so will have just three types of chocolate chip, and an orange scone, and lemon drops, and snickerdoodles, and…

Build a bakery of goods. Give your customers a reason to come back and shop for more.

Plus, you'll sometimes have a voracious reader come into your store. They'll want one of everything. Kind of exciting when that happens.

Release Content Regularly

Compare these two scenarios:

Publisher A publishes when they feel like it. They have no schedule. So in January, they publish a short story. Then nothing until May, when they suddenly publish fourteen different pieces.

Publisher B publishes according to a schedule. They publish every other week. Customers return regularly because they're guaranteed new content. In addition, they don't forget about Publisher B in between times.

Publishing content on a regular basis is another way to passively market your content.

Perhaps your life is too busy to publish once a month, or even once a quarter. Still, make sure that you have some kind of regular update, so that customers don't forget about you.

What day of the week you publish is no longer as important as just making sure that you regularly publish. Big publishers used to only publish on Tuesdays. Now, they publish books pretty much every day of the week.

Non-Fungible

Fungible is a term that is usually applied to goods and measures whether you can replace one of that kind of good with another. For example, a dollar's worth of pennies is fungible, and can be replaced with a single dollar bill.

Books are *non-fungible*. Readers don't easily accept one for another. If a reader likes romance, and is in the mood for a sweet, light romance, a book by Steven King is not going to fit the bill, no matter how popular or prevalent his books are.

So when you start thinking about actively marketing your books, you need to realize that not every book gets the same marketing treatment.

Let me put it this way—would you market a wedding cake the same way you would market a loaf of French bread? They're different items. They serve different functions in your bakery.

As a small press, you have limited time and resources. As a publisher, you need to decide which books get a push and which don't.

If you find yourself saying, *but all my books are special and desire a lot of attention!* you need to take off your writing hat and put back on your publishing hat.

Yes, all books are special. However, again, remember, you have *limited time and resources.* You must pick and choose.

NOTE: If you're only writing and publishing once book per year, there maybe other things you need to address. See Business for Breakfast, Volume 1, Chapter Eleven, What's Stopping You From Writing?

How do you pick which books get more attention? It's going to depend on the title you're publishing as well as what is right for *your* business. Remember, your publishing empire is different than everyone else's.

In this example, suppose you're writing a trilogy and this is the second book. Your plan is to publish the third book in six months.

Do you want to push the second book? Or do you just want to give the second book a small push, and dedicate a lot more time and energy to pushing the third book when it comes out and the trilogy is complete?

Usual wisdom is to not do much with a second book. But maybe it's Christmas-themed, and you're publishing it in November. So perhaps you do want to do more with this book.

For the third book in a trilogy, how much do you want to push it, versus now going back and doing a big push on book number one instead?

Maybe you write a lot of series, and this is a stand-alone book in a new genre. Are you planning on writing a lot more in that genre? Is this an area you plan on branching out into? Or is this a one-off?

All of these factors come into play when you're making the decision about what to in terms of active marketing for a book.

But…Then What?

There are whole degrees in marketing and advertisement. What you need to remember are two key things:

- Marketing is all about placing the right book in front of the right customer at the right time.
- Not all books are the same.

So who is your audience? How do readers who read your kind of genre discover new writers? How do they find the books they read?

I know, I know, it's chicken-and-egg. You're just starting out, you don't have any readers yet! If I have readers, they've already discovered me!

There are many ways to actively get your books in front of the right readers, including but not limited to:

- Purchasing an ad in a magazine
- Producing advanced paper copies of your books and sending them to reviewers
- Participating in a book bundle (where other authors' readers might discover you)
- Purchasing space in a newsletter, such as Fussy Librarian or Bookbub
- Sending out postcards to specialty bookstores

- Joining a group of writers and producing something cooperative so that you're each advertising each other, such as Book View Café or the Uncollected Anthology.
- Having the author send out a newsletter to his or her fans
- Doing a Goodreads giveaway
- Creating a contest around the books
- Sending out a publishing newsletter
- Buying an ad in your local movie theatre
- Doing a blog tour

Are there other roads to discoverability? Absolutely. Which one is right for your publishing business and this particular book? I can't tell you. No one can. You get to decide for yourself what is appropriate or not appropriate. Plus, you get to change your mind later.

NOTE: For a great book on this topic, see Discoverability by Kristine Kathryn Rusch.

Return on Investment

You'll hear this term used a lot: *return on investment*, or ROI.

In order to measure what *return* you're getting regarding a piece of marketing, you need to understand what it is that you want to accomplish with a particular marketing technique.

For example, what if you handed out fourteen paper copies of your book? And it only resulted in three paper sales? That would be a lousy return, right?

Except perhaps that wasn't your goal. Maybe you handed out those paper copies of your book in exchange for reviews. So you got three reviews for fourteen books (which is a very large return, quite honestly.) And those reviews garnered other reviews, and more electronic sales?

Now would you consider it a good return on investment?

Again, you must know what you're measuring in order to judge the return.

NOTE: For more information on this topic, see Discoverability by Kristine Kathryn Rusch.

Continually Hustling

Even with my publishing hat on, I don't think about marketing myself. It's foreign to my worldview.

As a writer, I don't push my books. It makes me uncomfortable.

Then I started publishing my fiancé's books. I also started making book business cards. The front of the business card has the cover of a book, the back has a shortened blurb, along with purchasing information.

These cards are the same size and shape as a standard business card. I personally feel that makes them look more professional, as opposed to cards with a more artistic size or cut.

When I first created these, I figured I'd never hand them out.

However, I live in a city. I go out a lot. And my fiancé has shown me just how easy it is to hand out business cards to people. To a waiter. To a barista. To the lady who runs the dry cleaner business. I put them up on bulletin boards, community boards, the board at my bank.

I've gone through stacks of one-hundred business card.

My fiancé, who is a more natural marketer, is constantly hustling his books, as well as handing out business cards.

What is the ROI? I think for the first batch of cards, it was minimal. However, we're so accustomed to ads, that we don't act the first time we see something. Or the second. Or the third. Maybe by the fourth time.

Has handing out cards (and we're on our fourth and fifth sets of different book cards at this point) increased awareness in my neighborhood as well as sales? It appears to be.

Plus, they make great party favors.

The one thing to caution you on: My fiancé is charming. He also backs right down if someone says, "I don't read X." If you do try the continual hustling approach, you must know when to walk away, or you'll just end up irritating people.

In Conclusion

Here are the three things you need to remember about marking, part two:

- Books are non-fungible. Each one deserves its own special marketing push, or not. It's completely up to you.
- Know what you're measuring when you do more active marketing.
- If you're continually hustling, know when to back down.

CHAPTER SIX

The Production Schedule is Written in Pencil

A production schedule should be developed for every project. This way, you'll have a good idea of what you're publishing and when.

But where does a production schedule start? Where does it end? And what are all the steps between manuscript and finished project?

I'm going to start with the finished project and move forward, accumulating dates. You can, however, move backwards: Pick a date by which you want to have something published, then work backwards figuring out your dates. I wouldn't advise doing this unless you have a lot of lead time, or are already familiar enough with your publishing schedule that you know where you can fudge things.

This chapter is going to get into more of the details of publishing, as well as building your own Checklist O'Doom.

Production—The Start

When does a book go into the production process? That's something that you'll get to decide for yourself.

Some publishers start with the beta or first reader. The writer has done their best to write a great book. Now it's time for an outside reader to point out where they got confused, where they cheered for the villain, where they laughed out loud, and perhaps where they started cursing the writer because it was two o'clock in the morning and they couldn't put the damned book down.

NOTE: I am NOT advising you to send your work to a critique group. See Business for Breakfast, Volume 1, Chapter Seven, Self-Confidence 101 for the differences between critique and first readering.

For novels, I generally allow two months for the first reader phase: One month for the readers to read, and a second month for me to think about things and incorporate comments.

It generally doesn't take me that long to incorporate comments. But sometimes other projects are in the way, and I can't get to the comments immediately. Two months gives me a good cushion.

You get to decide what's right for your business and process. Maybe the whole first reader step only takes a month—readers get two weeks and the writer gets two weeks.

But mark those dates down, as well as add *first reader* to your checklist.

Copyedits

I try to *always* send everything I write to a copyeditor. I have misspelled my own name before. I mix up words like "lie" and "lay," "further" and "farther." I need a good copyeditor to go through and clean up things.

Good copyeditors are busy people. This is another reason why I tend to give the first reading process two months: I can then give the copyeditor a firm date two months out for when I will need her services.

I can't just expect to finish something and drop it on her desk. She also has a very long lead time and schedule.

What if your favorite copyeditor isn't available in two months? He's gotten so popular that now he needs four months lead time?

Then you have a business decision to make. Do you continue to use this copyeditor, and adjust your publishing schedule? Or do you ask for suggestions and find another?

This is part of why the publishing schedule is always written in pencil.

As a publisher, I've developed relationships with three different copyeditors: my main two, plus a backup. If you're sending a lot of material out, you might consider doing the same.

Add *send to copyeditor* to your checklist.

How long do your copyedits generally take? I write fairly clean copy. By the time it goes to the copyeditor there really aren't that many mistakes for her to correct. So I get my material back in two weeks or less. But sometimes it takes a month, particularly with longer novels.

Another date to add to your calendar, plus you need to add *copyedits returned* to your checklist.

How long will it take you to incorporate the copyedits? Again, since I write fairly clean copy, I generally give myself two days. It takes that long for me in part because I'm trying to learn: I look at every comment and figure out why it's there, what it was she fixed, so the next time, I won't do it again.

How long it takes your writer is really going to depend on you, your process, and the particular project.

Yet another date to add to your calendar, as well as adding *incorporate copyedits* to your checklist.

Covers

Perhaps while you're waiting for your first readers to get back to you, you can create your cover or covers. Or maybe you'll create your covers while the book is with the copyeditor.

Or perhaps you're hiring out, having someone else create the covers for you.

However your covers get created, you need to have them finished before you can start formatting your book.

Add *create covers* to your checklist. You may want to break that down into *create ebook cover, create print cover, create audio cover, create business card cover*, etc.

I'm a member of a publishing cooperative, Book View Café. One of the wonderful things about being a member is that I can post the covers I design to the forums there and get critique and commentary from other professionals.

This cover review is also something I build into my schedule, generally about a weeks' worth of back and forth. If someone else is creating your cover, make sure you build review time into the schedule.

You may want to form your own group of professionals for critiquing covers. I would suggest putting up a cover (regardless of who created it) and merely asking, "What genre is this book?" Until you really understand genre, the answers may surprise you. Keep trying. Keep learning.

Add *cover review* to your checklist.

Different platforms take different cover sizes. Facebook prefers a particular image size. Amazon takes another. You may develop your own specific cover size for your website. And you may decide to do a smaller cover for inclusion in your ebooks.

NOTE: The different websites may or may not require a different size. They'll just crop the picture for you. Therefore your final version will look odd. It's better to learn the different sizes preferred by the different platforms and create them, so that way your covers all look the same.

Also, is this book going to be electronic only? Will you need to develop a print version? As well as an audio version? They all have their own requirements.

Add *generate different cover sizes* to your checklist.

Blurbs

If you're creating a print edition of your book, you'll need the blurb at this time, to add to the cover.

For me, it doesn't take me that long to write the first blurb. However, I generally throw it out and end up writing a second one. Or I tighten the first one significantly. None of it takes a lot of time. I do find, though, that I iterate on blurbs, improving them every time I touch them.

So creating a blurb needs to go on your checklist. You might also want to give yourself time to iterate and improve on a blurb.

Plus, you may need to develop a short blurb, a long blurb, a book tag, etc.

Add *create short blurb, long blurb, book tag, author tag* to your checklist.

Formatting

WARNING: Technology changes rapidly. What I have written in this section is current as of spring 2018. By summer, it may have changed.

You will need to generate at the very least an ebook, and possibly a print book as well.

You can hire someone to do your formatting for you. You can take the time to learn how to do it yourself. You may end up using an online service.

Learning how to format a book yourself will take some time. However, the tools have improved so it's *much* easier now.

Because I format a *lot* of books, and I have a technical background, it doesn't take me that long.

Add *format book* to your checklist.

Vellum

If you are formatting books on a regular basis, you will want to get the program Vellum. (No, they don't pay me for recommending them.)

Though Vellum only works on a Mac, it is worth picking up a refurbished Mac computer just to run Vellum on it. The program will save you that much time.

One of the huge advantages to Vellum is that you can create distributor-specific versions of your ebook. That means that someone who buys a version created for Nook will have only Nook links in their book. Someone who buys a Kindle book will have only links to other Kindle books, and so on.

In addition, Vellum also does print formatting. It isn't perfect. I won't use it on all books. But for most books, what the Vellum program produces for print is good enough.

There's a small learning curve for Vellum, and they keep improving the program all the times.

Online Formatting

If you are not formatting and publishing many books, you may choose to go with an online formatting solution in stead, such as the one offered by Draft2Digital (D2D).

I have never personally used one of the online formatting tools. However, I've been told by professionals that the output is gorgeous. YMMV. It is fast and easy, and perhaps you start there while saving up for a Mac computer.

However, I would rather have all the tools I need for the trade in my hands, rather than trust an online tool.

Print Formatting

For me, if I am NOT using Vellum, I format my print books using InDesign.

Formatting a print book takes longer than creating an ebook. I allow at least half a day of solid work to do a short book, two to three days for a longer book.

It isn't because it takes that much time to do the actual work. But I find my eyes get fuzzy if I work too long on a particular project, and I need to take breaks and go do something else for a while.

If I'm doing a print book, I automatically add six weeks to the schedule. Why?

Because you will need to view a printed proof of the book before you approve it. I am a small business, that means I want the cheapest shipping rate possible. Sometimes the service I use for print books (Createspace) can get me a proof in a week.

Sometimes, though, it takes two weeks. Particularly in November, when everyone is printing all their holiday books.

Then what happens if there's a mistake and I need to generate another proof? That's potentially another two weeks.

I can have something called *Extended Distribution* via Createspace. What this means is that my paper book will automatically display in the Barnes and Noble catalog, as well as the Kobo catalog, etc. without me doing a thing.

But it takes time for the book to show up in the extended distribution catalogs.

So I tend to approve the final Createspace print two weeks or more before I publish the electronic version.

Add *print formatting* to your checklist, as well as *uploading to distributor,* and *verifying printed proof.*

Categories and Keywords

The one last piece of information you need before you start publishing are the categories and keywords for your book. Spend an hour or more determining your keywords before you start publishing. Remember: the categories that different distributors, such as Amazon, change all the time. What was a valid category for the first book in a series may no longer exist by the time the fifth book rolls out. So you will need to do this step every time you publish something.

Add *determine categories and keywords* to your checklist.

For more on keywords and categories, see *Chapter Ten, Distributing and Branding.*

Price

What is the appropriate price for your book?

Believe it or not, that's also determined by genre. In some markets, like romance, readers won't pay a lot for their books, in part, because they read so many of them. In other markets, like mystery, readers expect to pay more for their books.

You need to spend another hour or more studying pricing for your genre.

Then add *determine the price* to your checklist.

Publish!

You've already set up all your accounts with the distributors. You've established your publishing date.

Now it's time to upload your files (which are all in a single, findable place, right?) As well as enter the description (again, your blurbs are all in a single, findable place, right?) And the keywords. And the cover.

The publishing process takes time, just because it does. Give yourself at least half a day to do it.

Add *Publish to distributors*, as well as the list of distributers that you're using on your checklist, so that you won't miss any.

And now, you're done! Right?

No, next comes the post-production phase, which I'll cover in the next chapter.

In Conclusion

Here are the three things to remember about the production schedule:

- The schedule can be long and complicated. Make a checklist.
- The checklist includes things like copyedits, generating all the different covers, formatting, picking a price, and publishing.
- Publishing to distributors is not the last step.

CHAPTER SEVEN

Post Production and Production Extras

The production process is finished! Your book has been uploaded to all the distributors.

Now what?

This chapter covers some of the post-production process, as well as some of the extras you may add to the production process itself.

Links

You'll need to wait a day, or two, or possibly three before your book will be "live" at the various distributor sites.

Once it goes live, remember that spreadsheet I talked about in *Chapter Two, Book Organization 101*? Use this spreadsheet to keep track of all the links to the various distributors.

You'll be using this spreadsheet in the next few steps.

You might want to add *add links* to your post-production checklist o'doom.

Notifications

So your book is live! Yay!

How are you going to tell the world?

Perhaps a Facebook announcement. And a blog post. And you'll add the information to your newsletter.

Guess what? You should add the links to where your book is available to that post or newsletter or what have you. (See why that spreadsheet is so important?)

Maybe as part of your marketing plan you've decided to create postcards that you're going to mail to specialty bookstores. Now would be the time to address them and do that.

Whatever other post production notifications that you want to do, make sure that you add them to your checklist. Or you'll forget to do them. Trust me on this.

Adding Marketing to the Schedule

The basic production schedule in the previous chapter didn't include any marketing. That's because the marketing you do for every book is going to be different, while the production list will stay roughly the same.

You may want to develop your own checklist of all the possible marketing things that you typically do, such as create business cards, create post cards, sign up for blog tours, do a Goodreads giveaway, run a Fussy Librarian campaign, create Amazon ads, etc.

Then add these dates to your production schedule, either pre- or post-production.

Advanced Reader Copies

Suppose that this book is getting a larger push. You've decided to create *advanced reader copies*, or ARCs. You send ARCs to traditional review venues, such as Booklist, Publisher's Weekly, Romantic Times, the Historic Novels Review, etc.

ARCs are generally done only as print books (there are currently a few exceptions). An ARC has a different cover than the final copy. It is clearly marked ADVANCED READER COPY. The back of an ARC generally contains marketing information, such as if you're going to be doing a blog tour, or radio appearances, or something else.

If you have never seen an ARC, go to a used bookstore and ask if they have any. You want to look at modern ones, which will have the actual cover, rather than the plain-bound, which are older.

Doing an ARC will push out your final publication date by several months. At this time, a site such as Publisher's Weekly requires that they receive the ARC four months *prior* to publication.

You see why the publication schedule is always written in pencil?

ISBNs and ARCs

An ARC should be its own special edition of a book. When creating the ARC, I recommend using the free Createspace ISBN for that version only. That way, you can approve the proof of the ARC and send it to as many people as you'd like. (Make sure that you don't select any distribution channels!)

When you approve the ARC, you have, in effect, "published" that book. The date you approve it becomes the official publication date for that book.

If you have a second ISBN for the final version of the book, you'll be able to have a more accurate publication date. This can be important when it comes to submitting a work for awards.

You should have the final ISBN number at the same time you create the ARC. Generally, that ISBN goes on the back cover of the ARC as part of the marketing material (along with the ISBN for the ebook.)

Once you produce the final version of the book, I would recommend going back in and unpublishing the ARC so that you can't accidentally send out copies of it when you intend to send out the final version.

Speed = Death

Publishing is a slow business. You can have a book ready, but because of reviews, edits, proofing, etc. it may not be available for sale for months.

You have to be okay with that as a publisher if you're going to do traditional marketing things.

Even if you're not doing traditional marketing things, it's still smart to build in time for people to review your work, your covers, your blurbs, your formatting.

Yes, you can go faster, but I wouldn't recommend it as part of your permanent workflow. You'll get burned out. Plus, the quality of your work will suffer.

Anytime you think you need to speed up, remember that in publishing, going too fast is generally a bad idea. Take the time to do everything right.

Plus, as a small business, you have to get used to the fact that you can't afford all the help you'll need, at least not right away. It will take time to build your business. Don't overstretch yourself (or your budget!)

When You Do Need It Now

There are times, though, when you do need to move quickly. For example, in early 2015, one of the books I had published "hit." It went from selling a few copies a day to selling hundreds.

The writer and I decided that the best sort of push we could give to this hit would be to publish the next in the series. Luckily, it was already half-written.

It was a matter of changing around the publishing schedule so we could publish the sequel next. As well as some other changes. (More about this in *Chapter Nine, What Happens When You Strike It Big?*)

By publishing the sequel early, that single "hit" sustained for quite some time. In addition, the sequel also "hit"—not to the same extent, but it continues to sell very well.

This was a case of being able to be nimble because I am a small press.

And this is another reason why the publishing schedule is always written in pencil.

Reviews

No, I'm not talking about external reviewers of your book. But the review that you must do, post-production.

A year from when you first published this book, you need to look at it again. Put it on your calendar, put it in your schedule, where ever it needs to go so you'll remember twelve months from now.

You'll have a year's experience under your belt at that point. You'll have learned an amazing amount of new things.

Is the book selling well? Great! You may not want to touch a thing.

Has the book not found its market? Or do you think it could be selling better?

Now is the time to look at the cover. You've spent the last year looking at genres and studying covers. Is the current cover all that it could be?

Look at the blurb. Does it need updating?

Look at the keywords and categories. Is the book sitting where it's supposed to be? Or does it need tweaking?

How about the price? Is the price still appropriate for this genre?

All of these things need to be reviewed on an annual basis, then measured against everything else you have on your plate.

Perhaps this is the first of a series. Maybe the entire series needs to be updated, rebranded. Or perhaps the third book in a trilogy is just about to come out, so you should revisit the first.

Or perhaps this was an odd, one-off book, and it's just fine for it to sit there and gather some weeds. You'll get to it next year. Or the year after that.

You have limited time and resources. Spend them appropriately.

In Conclusion

Here are the three things you need to remember about post production:

- Keep all your links to the various distributors in a separate spreadsheet.
- Add the marketing you're planning on doing to a

particular book to the production schedule. And always be prepared to change the final production date.

- Review your books at least once a year and make adjustments if necessary and appropriate for your business.

CHAPTER EIGHT

Contracts

I know, I know. Contracts can be scary things.

But they don't have to be long and complicated. They can be written in plain language. And they're really useful and necessary.

This chapter is going to talk about the most common contracts that you, as a publisher, will deal with, as well as some of the things you should be looking for.

NOTE: I am not a lawyer, nor do I play one on TV. Please do not construe this in any way, shape or form to constitute legal advice.

Why Sign Contracts?

As a general rule of thumb, remember that:

Anytime money changes hands, you should have a contract.

Why?

Contracts aren't for when things go right. They're for when things go wrong.

Contracts cover you in the worst case scenario.

As a writer and artist, you're used to thinking up worst case scenarios—more delicious ways to torture your protagonist.

Now apply those same skills to your business and your contracts.

Without a contract to spell out what is supposed to happen to the money coming in, what is the worst that can happen?

I hope I just gave you chills.

The good news is that you can create your own contracts, using plain language. Or do some searches on the internet for what you're trying to cover. There are lots of good templates out there that you can personalize.

If you're trying to do something fancy, contact a lawyer. If you live in a major city, there are often free law services for artists. (Lawyers are people too, you know.)

Just keep in mind that as a business, you need contracts.

Between the Writer and Publisher

Do you have a contract between you, the writer, and you, the publisher?

Even if you're not making much money, the *intent* is to make money. So there should be a simple contract between me, the writer, and me, the publisher.

What should such a contract cover?

Mine states things like:

- Publisher publishes the work and sells it.
- Writer gets a certain percentage of the sales.
- Writer has the right to examine the publisher's books, at the writer's expense. If there are accounting errors greater than 5%, the cost of the entire examination falls on the publisher.
- Writer shall provide publisher with photo and bio.
- How a writer can leave the publisher, and what happens at that time.

What goes into your contract is up to you. But consider this scenario: You get famous. Then you get hit by a bus. Your cousin Mike McGreedy takes over your publishing business. Your heirs plan to live on your writing income.

If there's *no contract*, Mike McGreedy doesn't have to pay your heirs a dime.

Money is changing hands between your publishing company and you, the writer.

Make sure you have a contract that covers that.

Work For Hire

As a publisher, after my writing contracts, the most frequent type of contract that I sign is *work for hire*. This contract covers exactly what you think it covers: when you hire someone to do work for you.

What kind of work? Covers, for example. Or editing. Perhaps ebook or print formatting. All of these are considered work for hire. You don't pay a percentage to them. It isn't ongoing. Once the project is finished, they go their own way.

What should be in a work for hire contract? Remember, I'm not a lawyer and this isn't legal advice. But I look for the following in a work for hire contract:

- What exactly am I purchasing? What am I getting?
- Who owns the intellectual property? Generally, the writer should own the intellectual property. (It can get more complicated with covers—for example, you may merely license the artwork for a cover, though you'll own the *design* of the cover. You need to pay attention to this.)
- What is the draft/review process?
- What is the cost?
- What is the kill fee, if any?
- What is the relationship between the parties? (There should be a paragraph stating that this is work for hire, and you're not hiring an employee.)
- If I'm dealing with confidential information, what does the non-disclosure portion of the contract look like?
- When is the contract terminated?

Spend the time to read your contracts. Remember, they aren't there for when something goes rights. Contracts cover you when something goes horribly, horribly wrong.

Terms of Service

The next type of contract that I, as a publisher, sign regularly are the terms of service agreements that you must click through on every web site.

Before you signed up for a distribution service, did you take the time to read their terms of service? If you haven't, go do so now. And get in the habit of reading these regularly.

There are some services that I cannot recommend, based solely on their terms of service. The biggest thing to watch for: *who owns your intellectual property?*

There are social media sites, like Facebook, that explicitly state that they own any intellectual property that you post. If you're posting snippets of your work, Facebook now owns them.

(I am not a lawyer, nor do I ever want to be one. Think of this scenario though: what happens if you posted chapters of your work frequently on Facebook? Then you became famous? Facebook can now repost those chapters *without paying you* as part of their advertisement. And there is nothing you can do about it. Courts have been upholding terms of service as a legally binding contract. It doesn't matter if you read the terms of service or not before you clicked. The court assumes that you did.)

The second thing that you need to watch for is: *when and how can the service change their terms?* Can they change them at any time without notification? Or must they notify you?

One of the reasons why I continue to use Createspace is because they have understandable terms of service. Lightning Source, at least as of March, 2015, has an extremely convoluted terms of service for small presses (128 pages worth!) In addition, they *never* explicitly state that I own my own intellectual property.

Get in the habit of reading those terms of service. You're a business dealing with other businesses. And look at them in terms of worst case scenario.

NOTE: As of March 2018, Lightning Source had updated their contracts and some of them are now usable. But I still, personally, don't trust them.

Other Services Contracts

As opposed to work for hire, which has a finite time, service contracts are ongoing. Beyond terms of service that you sign for websites, you might not deal with many service contracts.

Service contracts may include a webhost or web master, who manages your website for you. Maybe you have a financial person, who organizes all your various distribution reports into one easy-to-read Excel spreadsheet.

A lot of what to look for in work for hire contracts remains for service contracts. However, the *how does this end* part becomes critical for service contracts. What happens when you cancel the service? Who keeps what? You need to make sure those types of things are in your contract.

In Conclusion

Here are the three things to remember about contracts:

- There should be a contract covering every time money changes hands.
- Contracts protect you when things go wrong.
- Read the terms of service for every web site you work with.

CHAPTER NINE

What Happens When You Strike It Big?

Early in 2015, one of the books that my small press publishes struck it big. Or at least, bigger than anything else I'd published to date.

We went from selling a few copies every day to selling hundreds. Then, it happened again in fall of 2017.

Consider this chapter a case study in what happens when suddenly something takes off, and what we did (both right and wrong!) as well as future plans.

The Story

I'll state this up front: I don't check my book sales numbers every day. What's the point? It's just data, and it's distracting. There isn't anything I'm going to do with that information. So I don't bother.

However, I had just published something else and was checking the status on that book. While I was in the Amazon dashboard, I thought I'd check sales. I hadn't for more than a week.

Holy cow.

The line of sales had gone almost completely vertical.

I looked at the generated report and found out that it was a single title, one of my fiancé's books—a novella.

To this day, we have no idea what happened to make it suddenly "pop." It's got a good cover—but so do all the books I publish. It has a good blurb—again, ditto. It was science fiction, so perhaps it was genre related.

The only change we'd made was in the previous week—which was to place it in the appropriate categories.

Was that why it popped? Possibly. However, we really don't know why. People talk about the Amazon 90-day machine. Perhaps it was that. We've hit it twice, now.

Flail

Seriously. I think for the next couple of days I, as the publisher, as well as my fiancé, the writer, just flailed and freaked. We kept asking ourselves, *is this really happening?*

Sales continued to climb. It wasn't a single day fluke.

We continued to flail and freak.

Celebrate

Celebrate this success in a manner that is meaningful for you.

For us, we went out to a really nice dinner with a half bottle of wine and ate and drank and flailed and freaked.

But we celebrated as well. Neither of us trusted this bit of good luck that had shown up out of the blue.

We did a similar celebration the second time. We'd also learned from experience not to trust it. While the current rise in income was great, we knew that it could disappear just as quickly as it had shown up.

Strike While The Iron Is Hot

While that property was in the top ten of the Amazon best seller lists we started making plans and figuring out what to do next.

Some of it was obvious: we got into Fussy Librarian. That made a difference in sales.

NOTE: As of spring 2018, there are so many of the smaller services, their effect has diluted. I wouldn't recommend them as of now.

We decided to branch into audio with the hot selling property. We went through the ACX program, doing a 50/50 royalty share with a producer. We were very lucky and got a fantastic producer.

Fortunately, my fiancé already had half of the sequel already written. He was able to finish it, I was able to edit it, create a cover, and publish it as well.

Which led to another bump in sales.

We rearranged the publishing schedule.

He'd written and completed one novel, that was a stand-alone, that we were planning on publishing first. Instead, he finished a second novel, that was set in the same universe, that we published first instead. (Remember, the publishing schedule is always written in pencil.)

The Writing Comes First

While my fiancé was very happy to finish the sequel as well as the other novel, as a publisher, I would have understood if he'd pushed back and said that he needed to finish something else first. We would have made other plans.

But he was happy to switch gears and write more in the universe that was selling.

Because after we finished flailing and freaking out, we both got back to the writing, which is always the most important thing.

Writers write. They don't just check Amazon numbers and stats and dream about what might come.

If this happens to you, there may be a time of flailing. I know we sure did.

But sooner or later (and hopefully it's sooner) you get back to the writing.

We followed through with this both the first time as well as the second time. You need to keep writing. Don't let the marketing department into your writing office. Just keep doing the things you've been doing.

Bakery

In *Chapter Five, Basic Marketing, Part Two* I talked about your publishing house as a bakery, and how you had to publish the next thing, so that customers could come back, and keep coming back for more.

This success happened for my fiancé at the right time in many ways. He already had a bakery of goods available. He had three collections of short stories, as well as all the short stories published individually. I'd also published some poetry of his. He had more than one novella available. Everything was properly categorized, as well as had good covers, good blurbs, good branding, etc.

Because he had a bakery, we've had more than one voracious reader come through and just pick one of everything. Even the poetry has been selling, which was kind of astonishing.

If he'd had this success with a single item in his bakery, we wouldn't have seen the halo effect of more sales as readers spread out through the rest of his books.

Mistakes

When you have a piece that's selling *don't touch it.*
We made that mistake.

Sales tanked the day I made changes to the metadata for that piece. The sales did pick right back up the following day. However, the day we messed with the book were some of our lowest sales for the next two months.

Even if there's a typo in the description, leave it.

If you must update a title (for example, you are publishing the sequel) make sure that the day you mess with it is the day when you have the least sales. For us, his sales rhythm almost looks like a heartbeat. Sales are worst on Tuesdays and Wednesdays, then they gain speed and climb, with Sundays generally being our best days. Mondays drop off, then Tuesdays drop down further.

Also remember that the majority of book sales (not just electronic, but all book sales) occur between midnight and three AM. This includes fiction as well as non-fiction. If you must mess with a title, do it early in the morning, not late at night.

We followed this advice the second time lightning struck, and only updated the books when it appeared to be the slowest time for sales, which had changed to Mondays for the second spike.

Newsletter

Because of the success of that one novella, my fiancé now has a good-sized audience for his newsletter.

NOTE: The newsletter was already set up and ready to take subscribers before anything hit. Along with a static website. Assume success. Plan for victory.

We send out thank you notes to everyone who subscribes. Early subscribers also received free fiction.

With the newsletter, he is going to be able to get people interested in the novel (which will be coming out a couple months after this book is finished).

His newsletter subscribers has continued to grow and he puts out a regular quarterly newsletter, always with some sort of "prize" for his readers buried at the bottom.

Pre-Orders

Because of the interest in the first piece, as well as the newsletter, I made his first novel available for pre-order through Amazon, Kobo, and iTunes. I haven't had a lot of pre-orders, but I do have some.

As of March 2018, I now put almost everything up via pre-order. Some books we have a tremendous number of pre-orders, other, we have none. I never put an incomplete book up for pre-order—it's always the complete, finished book.

Website

Before this hit, my fiancé's website, while already established, was fairly static.

With the hit, he started improving his website, adding more material about the universe and series and characters. He started blogging regularly. He engages with fans on Facebook as well as his website and through email.

As the publisher, I didn't push him to do any of this. It's something that, to his surprise, he actually enjoys. It makes my job easier to have an author doing some of the promotion.

Contracts

He already had a contract with my publisher. We have renegotiated that to pay for some of the extra services that my publisher will now provide, such as ads, email placement, events, etc.

Next Steps

Audible just gave us twenty-five codes that we can use to give the audio book away for free. We're going to be doing some giveaways using those as strategically as we can.

His first novel comes out in May. We're holding an event—mainly a party. I don't expect to sell many books. It's another celebration, and an important one.

My fiancé continues to have fun with his writing. I, as the publisher, make sure that I give him the space and encouragement he needs to keep writing.

Social Media

Since the first big "hit", my now-husband has a regular presence on Facebook. He blogs once a week and is always chatting with his fans. His posts are rarely "buy my book" but instead about the worlds he's built or the research he's done, or even, "Here's a cool new thing that you should know about." I believe that because his Facebook feed is so genuine, he attracts genuine people and fans.

In Conclusion

Here are the three things you need to remember from this single case study:

- Books can pop at any time.
- Prepare for success. Make sure that you have all the infrastructure in place when something does pop. Assume success. Plan for victory.
- Get back to writing.

CHAPTER TEN

Distribution and Branding

This chapter is going to get into more of the nitty gritty of distributing your work, as well as some general branding topics.

Amazon Keywords and Categories

NOTE: This information is current as of March 2018. Will it remain current? No. You need to verify what's current when you approach this.

The three most important things you can do to get the books you publish in front of the right readers are:

- Determine the genre.
- Get the most excellent cover you can.
- Write the most exciting blurb you can.

(All of these assume that you've already written a kick-ass book.)

The next step is to make sure that the book is published in the correct genre.

Categories and keywords are primarily used on the Amazon distribution platform. Other distributors may use keywords and categories, but at this time, Amazon is the only platform that uses them together. So all of the information in this section primarily applies to Amazon.

What is a Category?

A *category* is the top level genre that you can pick for Amazon. It's the bucket. The big container.

You can only pick two categories for Amazon.

I used to recommend picking the biggest categories you could. However, that backfired on me with some titles. Now, I go more specific for some titles (like for hard SF, military SF) and more general for other titles (like mine that straddle more than one genre).

When picking big categories, I tend to pick *fiction: general* for one of the categories, then I pick the primary genre for the second category, such as *science fiction: general* or *fantasy: general*.

Then I use keywords and keyword phrases to slot the book into the correct subcategories. At this time, Amazon only gives you seven entries for keywords. You can put up to four words into each slot.

How do you know what the keywords are? In the Kindle Direct Publishing help, there's a topic, Selecting Browse Categories. (https://kdp.amazon.com/help?topicid=A200PDGPEIOX41).

The tables in this help topic list many keywords. However, it is subject to change. Keep up to date with it.

However, you'll note that in my example, neither *military* or *space opera* show up as keywords. They are valid categories, however.

You need to explore the categories and subcategories and sub-subcategories on your own to find the niche that's right for your work.

More About Keywords

Amazon states that you have seven keywords.

What you actually have, as of March 2018, is seven keyword *phrases*. Amazon picks up four words between each of the six commas.

For example, I have a post-apocalyptic fairy tale. I use all four of those words between two commas. Amazon puts that novel into both post-apocalyptic as well as under fairy tales.

Experiment! It doesn't take that long for Amazon to republish a title.

Where Else to Find Those Categories

At the bottom of the sale page for a book on Amazon you'll find all the categories and subcategories that a work is slotted into. Make sure that you're looking at the Kindle version of a book—the categories and subcategories don't show up for print or audio versions.

Author and Series Branding

If you're lucky, you're just starting out, and are just starting to think about branding for both your author name, your genres, and your series. (Unlike some of us who had thirty titles up before we started getting consistent and had to go back and redo all those covers!)

Find a font that you like for the author's name that is appropriate for your genre. If you write in a lot of genres, you may want to consider different fonts for different genres. (You may want to use this same font on your author website.)

For my publishing house, I tend to use the same font and treatment for the author name with a few exceptions (for example, literary.)

However, I'll use a different font for the title depending on genre.

My fantasy titles tend to use one group of fonts. My science fiction uses a different set of fonts. Mystery, yet a different set.

This way, I'm branding by author and genre through the cover design. Readers may or may not be able to articulate what they're seeing. However, subconsciously, they'll recognize the brand.

In addition, if you write in a series, you should consider series branding. Use the same fonts for all the titles in the series. Maybe develop a bug or logo for that series. Label each book as part of that series, then use the same label (or something very similar) for each book.

When you publish a book in a series, make sure that you mark it as such. Many of the distributors let you indicate that a book is part of a series.

Series Publishing Schedule

Because of the wonderful new world that we live in, an author can now write all the books in a series, then release them one after another, with perhaps only a month in between.

Some writers have had great success doing that.

HOWEVER.

It is your business, and your business decision, about when and how to publish a series. Maybe you publish them as they are finished, and there isn't a regular schedule.

What makes sense for you and your business? You get to decide that.

Web Basics—Branding

Some of this was covered earlier in *Chapter One, Initial Decisions*. This is just a basic checklist for you, the publisher, to make sure that your writer has done to maximize their web presence and increase their brand.

- Amazon Central Author Page. Make sure that this gets set up, and that all of the author's books are claimed.

For extra credit, find and set up an Amazon Author Page in every other country they sell into, such as Japan, Germany, etc.

Even if you have decided not to use Amazon as a distributor, you should still set up an Amazon Author page with a link to where readers *can* find your books.

- Goodreads Author Page. Again, make sure that this gets

set up and that all of the author's books are in the Goodreads system.

- Facebook page. The author doesn't have to have a large presence on Facebook. They must be findable.

Why? Publishing is an international business. Suppose a German publisher reads one of your author's books, falls in love with it, and decides to do a German translation of it.

How will they find you? They won't contact the publisher. They will contact the writer. They may or may not try an internet search (and find the author's web page.) They may, instead, just use Facebook to find your author.

- Author Website

The author website can be either a static website, or it can be updated frequently. It depends on the author.

In Conclusion

Here are the three things you need to remember about distribution and branding:

- Get a great cover and blurb first. Then make sure you are using the correct categories and keywords.
- Make sure your authors have some level of web presence so that both their readers and other publishers can find them.
- Start developing branding now, not just for your authors but for genre and series.

CHAPTER ELEVEN

Formatting

This chapter will get into more of the details of formatting book for distribution.

Ebook—Interior Basics

Don't worry about specifying a font when you create an ebook. All ebook readers allow the user to choose the font they want to read in. They can also change the size of the font, so you can never be certain where an item is going to fall on a page.

Your ebook should contain a title page that also lists the author.

You may want to make the copyright information its own page. Make sure to include that the work is copyrighted by the author.

I always list that the interior design is copyrighted by my publisher. (Remember, you copyright a *form* of something. If you don't understand that, I would recommend starting with *The Copyright Handbook: What Every Writer Needs to Know* by Stephen Fishman.) I generally also list a copyright for the cover design.

As part of the copyright information at the front of the book, I include information about signing up for a writer's newsletter. (This will be repeated later.)

Most ebook conversion programs automatically generate a table of contents, so you don't need to create one.

I generally move all other information about the book—such as a list of character, author notes and acknowledgements, etc. to the back of the book. That way, when a reader samples the book, they get a good chunk of text, not the nice-to-have information.

At the end of the ebook, I put in any appropriate links (such as if this book is part of a series, I put in a link to the next book).

I also add three sections—about the author, also by the author, and about the publisher.

In the About the Author section, I put in a second call to never miss a release and sign up for the writer's newsletter. (No one signs up for a newsletter the first time they see a notice about it. But they may be more inclined the second time they see it.) Especially if they liked the book they just finished.

I also ask for reviews in a very polite way.

After the About the Publisher section, I add any ads that are appropriate, for books that aren't in the same series but are related.

Verifying Your Ebook

One of the advantages of working with a cooperative book publisher is that there are a lot of members who have a lot of different devices. All ebooks published by Book View Café are looked at on at least seven different combinations of devices and readers.

Not every publisher has access to that sort of resource. However, you need to page through your ebooks on as many different devices as you can.

Print—Interior Basics

When I am doing a basic book, I will use Vellum to create the print interior. It's fast, easy, and I use the same source files for creating the ebooks as I do the print books.

However, you can't control everything in Vellum. Sometimes it just doesn't produce a print book that's good enough.

Then, I must switch to a program from Adobe called InDesign for creating my print books. At one point, InDesign was the industry standard.

It is possible to create the interior of a print book using Word or some other word processor. I won't—it will take you so much time, and it's possible you won't achieve the results you want.

If you're serious about publishing, I would recommend getting InDesign in addition to getting Vellum.

Like many other things, the design of book interiors changes. It's also dependent on genre. You need to go and look at brand new books in a bookstore to get a feel for what's new, how interiors have changed, keep changing.

Because I use Word for creating my text, then InDesign, I tend to use Word styles. A *style* is where you specify what something looks like. Word comes with some styles already, such as Heading1, Normal, etc. I generally add at least one other, for the scene separator.

Because I use those styles in the Word document, they flow directly into the InDesign document. This makes it very easy to make any changes to the text—all I have to do is change the style.

In general, for a fiction book, I would recommend the following for the front matter. Note that these start with a right-hand page, and are continuous—right-hand followed by a left-hand page.

- Teaser from the book, that invites the reader to continue
- Copyright page
- Fancy title page, with the publishing house logo
- Less fancy title page, that the author can use for signing
- Blank page
- Any author notes, dedication, character lists, etc. (As many pages as necessary)
- Blank pages as necessary
- Start of book (start on a right-hand page.)

Pick an easy to read font for the body text. Remember that what shows up on the screen generally will look larger than when it's printed on the page, so you might want to go with something smaller than you think will work.

Pay attention to how the font makes you feel. It's been said that fonts are the clothes that the words wear. The wrong font can make you angry. It's a visceral reaction. Pay attention and change the font if it bothers you.

For your headers and footers—keep in mind how a reader reads a book—from the top left corner down to the bottom right. If you put text or a page number or something in that upper left hand corner, you may be bumping the reader out of the story every time they turn the page. So keep readability in mind.

One of the ways that I try to enhance the reader experience is by matching the font used for the title on the cover with the font used for the title inside the book. Sometimes this isn't possible—the cover font won't work on the interior. I still choose a font that's close.

Remember also that your print book will be bound. You want the interior margin to be big enough that the reader can read the start of every sentence without having to crack the spine.

Again, this is the time you can go wild with the scene separators, additional art at the start of every chapter, etc. Have fun with it!

For the end, I tend to put an About the Author page, with an About Knotted Road Press page. If there are any ads, I put them after the publisher page.

And again, on both the copyright page as well as the About the Author page I put in a reminder about signing up for the newsletter.

After you finish creating the PDF, make sure that you get one (or more!) printed proofs. What you see on your screen and what you'll see on the page are often very different. Take the time to look at an actual printed copy.

In Conclusion

Here are the three things to remember about formatting:

- Don't worry about the font for an ebook. Be concerned instead about the size and weight of a font.
- Make the print readable. And get a proof copy.
- Be sure to include ways for readers to connect with the author, such as a newsletter.

CHAPTER TWELVE

In Conclusion

In this volume of *Business for Breakfast* I've tried to give an overview, with some details, about being a professional publisher. I've tried to cover the basics.

You should have some idea of the business of publishing. Not all the details—those change too frequently. You can easily find those on your own.

There are a lot of advanced topics that I didn't cover. For example, developing your own list of reviewers who you send your work to. Or creating a catalog of books, that you can send to bookstores. Or joining the American Booksellers Association (ABA) and using their services to target booksellers. Possibly using Createspace to print the interiors of a book, then using a local printer to create hardbacks.

There are so many more things you can do as a publisher. Getting into library systems. Forming your own cooperative. Selling at conventions. Purchasing ad space.

Creating collections and anthologies. Using Kickstarter for a project. Creating more detailed sales plans. Creating a detailed business plan for your small press.

If you're serious about publishing, find other small press publishers you can talk with. Exchange ideas and plans, and maybe barter some—if you're a wiz at interiors, and maybe some other publisher is a wiz at marketing plans, maybe you can trade.

So keep studying. Keep learning. The world of publishing continues to change. You'll need to change with it.

See you 'round the breakfast table.

Leah

APPENDIX

Recommended Reading List

There are lots of good books out there. Here are some suggestions.

Daily, Frederick W. *Tax Savvy for Small Business. NOLO, 2013.*

Fishman, Stephen. *The Copyright Handbook: What Every Writer Needs To Know. NOLO, 2014.*

Levine, Mark. *The Fine Print of Self-Publishing. Bascom Hill Publishing Group, 2014.*

Mancuso, Anthony. *Incorporate Your Business: A Legal Guide to Forming a Corporation in Your State. NOLO, 2013.*

Rusch, Kristine Kathryn. *Discoverability. WMG Publishing, 2015.*

Sedwick, Helen. *Self-Publisher's Legal Handbook. Ten Gallon Press, 2014.*

In addition, I would recommend taking any of the workshops listed on this page:

http://www.deanwesleysmith.com/online-workshops/

These lectures are pretty good, too:

http://www.deanwesleysmith.com/lecture-series/

READ MORE!

Be sure to pick up the other books in the Business for Breakfast series!

The Beginning Professional Writer
The Beginning Professional Publisher
The Beginning Professional Storyteller
The Intermediate Professional Storyteller
Business Planning for Professional Publishers
The Healthier Professional Writer
The Three Act Structure

ABOUT THE AUTHOR

Leah R Cutter writes page-turning, wildly imaginative fiction in exotic locations, such as a magical New Orleans, the ancient Orient, Hungary, the Oregon coast, rural Kentucky, Seattle, Minneapolis, and many others.

She writes literary, fantasy, mystery, science fiction, and horror fiction. Her short fiction has been published in magazines like *Alfred Hitchcock's Mystery Magazine* and *Talebones*, anthologies like *Fiction River*, and on the web. Her long fiction has been published both by New York publishers as well as small presses.

Find Leah's books here.

Follow her blog at www.LeahCutter.com.

Never miss a release!

If you'd like to be notified of new releases, sign up for my newsletter.

I only send out newsletters once a quarter, will never spam you, or use your email for nefarious purposes. You can also unsubscribe at any time.

http://www.leahcutter.com/newsletter/

Reviews

It's true. Reviews help me sell more books. If you've enjoyed this story, please consider leaving a review of it on your favorite site.

ABOUT KNOTTED ROAD PRESS

Knotted Road Press fiction specializes in dynamic writing set in mysterious, exotic locations.

Knotted Road Press non-fiction publishes autobiographies, business books, cookbooks, and how-to books with unique voices.

Knotted Road Press creates DRM-free ebooks as well as high-quality print books for readers around the world.

With authors in a variety of genres including literary, poetry, mystery, fantasy, and science fiction, Knotted Road Press has something for everyone.

Knotted Road Press
www.KnottedRoadPress.com